INTRODUCTION

AF491299

THIS BOOK-'BEYOND CHRISTMAS' IS COMPILED FROM 'THE HOLY-BIBLE', (King James Version).

I dedicate this book to the one and only person on whom the whole history of this world is made. He is, <u>JESUS CHRIST-</u> <u>'The Son of The Living God-THE CREATOR'</u> of this beautiful Universe'.

<u>John-1:</u>

3. All things were made by Him; and without Him was not anything made that was made.

[His birth is the mark of the History of this world. '<u>Before Christ</u>' **BC** (Old Testament) and After His Birth as **AD** (an abbreviation for the Latin phrase **A**nno **D**omini, which means "<u>in the year of the Lord</u>") (New Testament). He was sent two thousand years ago by 'The Creator', to save us from the clutches of sin].

<u>John-17:</u>

3. And this is life eternal, that they might know thee <u>the only true God,</u> and Jesus Christ, whom thou hast sent.

1 John-4:

14. "And we have seen and do testify that the Father sent the Son to be the Saviour of the world."

[The selected verses aim to present the truth about JESUS CHRIST-THE SON of THE LIVING GOD, whose birth is celebrated throughout the world as **'CHRISTMAS'.**]

Psalms-100:

5. "For the LORD is good; His mercy everlasting; and His truth endureth to all generations."

[HE IS **THE TRUE GIFT** to this world from THE FATHER-Almighty GOD-THE CREATOR.]

James-1:

17. Every good gift and every perfect gift is from above, and cometh down from the Father of lights, with whom is no variableness, neither shadow of turning.

2 Corinthians-9:

15. "Thanks be unto God for His unspeakable gift."

<u>PREFACE</u>

<u>1 Kings-8:</u>

60. "That all the people of the earth may know that the LORD is God, and that there is none else."

[This compilation is all about the **<u>sacrifice</u> of both The Father-The Creator,** who loves His creation with everlasting love <u>and</u> **The Son's, obedience** to His Father.**]**

<u>Romans-5:</u>

8. But God commendeth His love toward us, in that, while we were yet sinners, Christ died for us.

9. Much more then, being now justified by His blood, we shall be saved from wrath through Him.

[The Son glorified 'His Father', by offering Himself to fulfill His plan for us].

<u>John-3:</u>

17. For God sent not His Son into the world to condemn the world; but that the world through Him might be saved.

Romans-5:

19. "For as by one man's disobedience many were made sinners, so by the obedience of one shall many be made righteous.

John-10:

17. Therefore doth my Father love me, because I lay down my life, that I might take it again.

[In today's fast-paced world, it's easy to find ourselves caught up in the hustle and bustle of life. <u>We may claim to be Christians</u>, attending church from time to time, perhaps saying a quick prayer before meals, and even dropping an occasional 'God bless you' in conversations, but….

<u>Are we truly living as GOD intended us to?</u>]

1 John-2:

<u>3. And hereby we do know that we know Him, if we keep His commandments.</u>

Ephesians-4:

32. And be ye kind one to another, tenderhearted, forgiving one another even as God for Christ's sake hath forgiven you.

<u>BEYOND CHRISTMAS</u>

[Christmas is not just going to church or wearing new-clothes or wine and dine. It is not one day celebration, <u>It is beyond that.</u>]
It is 'The LOVE expressed by GOD-The Father-CREATOR through His Son-JESUS CHRIST' to redeem us from the devil-the deceiver. <u>It is "THE EVERLASTING LOVE for EVERLASTING LIFE".</u>

<u>John-3:</u>

16. For God so loved the world, that He gave His only begotten Son, that whosoever believeth in Him should not perish, but have everlasting life.

<u>1 John-3</u>:

8. He that committeth sin is of the devil; for the devil sinneth from the beginning. <u>For this purpose the Son of God was manifested, that He might destroy the works of the devil.</u>

John-14:

6. "Jesus saith unto him, I am the way, the truth, and the life: no man cometh unto the Father, but by me. "

[By, following the <u>Manual</u> of GOD-ALMIGHTY (<u>instructions-commandments-statutes</u>.)]

<u>John-12:</u>

47. And if any man hear my words, and believe not, I judge him not: For I came not to judge the world, but to save the world.

[<u>'Creator-God Almighty', sent 'Jesus Christ' to end the sacrifice</u> (which was required from us human called- sin offering)<u> because there was no remorse or repentance in that act</u>].

<u>1 John-2:</u>

2<u>. "And he is the propitiation for our sins: and not for ours only, but also for the sins of the whole world."</u>

<u>1 John-5:</u>

17. "All unrighteousness is sin: and there is a sin not unto death."

<u>Psalms-51:</u>

5. Behold, I was shapen in iniquity; and in sin did my mother conceive me."

<u>Romans-6:</u>

23. <u>The wages of sin is death;</u> but the gift of

God is eternal life through Jesus Christ our Lord.

1 John-5:

11. *And this the record, that God hath given to us eternal life, and this life is in His Son.*

[This world is blinded by the devil-the deceiver, who is a fallen angel].

2 Corinthians-4:

4. *In whom the god of this world hath blinded the minds of them which believe not, lest the light of the glorious gospel of Christ, who is the image of God, should shine unto them.*

[Sin separates GOD and man, it brings disobedience to His words and blinds us.The core of the true gospel is to call sinners to repentance. Sin brings pain.]God Almighty sent His son to feel that real pain.]

1 John-3:

5. *And ye know that He was manifested to take away our sins; and in Him is no sin.*

Luke-13:

3. *I tell you, Nay: but, except ye repent, ye shall all likewise perish.*

<u>Luke-5:</u>

32. *"I came not to call the righteous, but sinners to repentance."*

<u>1 John-3:</u>

9. *Whosoever is born of God doth not commit sin; for His seed remaineth in him: and he cannot sin, because he is born of God.*

<u>John-8:</u>

51. *Verily, verily, I say unto you, If a man keep my saying, <u>he </u>shall never see death.*

<u>1 Peter-5:</u>

8. *"Be sober, be vigilant; because your adversary the devil, as a roaring lion, walketh about, seeking whom he may devour:"*

[The implicit obedience of Jesus Christ to His Father-Almighty-God's plan, made Him as '<u>The only celebrity of this world </u>and He was glorified by <u>His Father-The Creator-Almighty God</u>].

<u>John-8:</u>

29. <u>*"And he that sent me is with me: the Father hath not left me alone; for I do always those things that please him."*</u>

[It is not one day relationship, it is a continuous relationship with the Father-The CREATOR and with His Son-JESUS CHRIST]

1 John-4:

10. *Herein is love, not that we loved God, but that He loved us, and sent His Son to be the propitiation for our sins.*

1 Chronicles-16:

11. Seek the LORD and His strength, seek His face continually.

Matthew-28:

18. And Jesus came and spake unto them, saying, All power is given unto me in heaven and in earth.

1 John-5:

10. He that believeth on the Son of God hath the witness in himself: he that believeth not God hath made Him a liar; because he believeth not the record that God gave of His Son.

11. And this is the record, that God hath given to us eternal life, and this life is in His Son.

JESUS CHRIST

People are ignorant of the fact who **JESUS CHRIST IS,** It is clearly mentioned in **THE SCRIPTURE.**

HE IS THE SON OF THE LIVING GOD-THE ALMIGHTY' and this was prophesied in 'The Old-Testament', and is well explained by JESUS CHRIST Himself which is written in 'THE GOSPEL' of LUKE, JOHN of 'The New-Testament'.

Luke-24:

44. And He said unto them, These are the words which I spake unto you, while I was yet with you, that all things must be fulfilled, which were written in the law of Moses, and in the prophets, and in the psalms, concerning me.

45. Then opened He their understanding, that they might understand the scriptures,

John-5:

39. "Search the scriptures; for in them ye think ye have eternal life: and they are they which testify of me."

[We will see a brief history of JESUS CHRIST
1) Birth, 2) Life, 3) Death and 4) Resurrection and
what they mean to us]

HIS BIRTH; Humility; LIFE-An example for perfection;
DEATH-Sacrifice; Resurrection-Victory.]

Matthew-5:

5. *"Blessed are the meek: for they shall
inherit the earth."*

Matthew-5:

48. *"Be ye therefore perfect, even as your
Father which is in heaven is perfect."*

Hebrews-9:

26. *"For then must He often have suffered
since the foundation of the world: but now
once in the end of the world hath He
appeared to put away sin by the sacrifice of
Himself."*

Isaiah-25:

8. *"He will swallow up death in victory; and
the Lord GOD will wipe away tears from off
all faces; and the rebuke of His people shall
He take away from off all the earth: for the
LORD hath spoken it."*

1) <u>JESUS CHRIST'S BIRTH</u>

[It was prophesied in the Old-testament that the Saviour will be born of a virgin by 'The Holy Spirit' and it was fulfilled in the 'New-testament]

Isaiah-7:

14. *Therefore the Lord himself shall give you a sign; Behold, a virgin shall conceive, and bear a son, and shall <u>call-His name Immanuel</u>.*

Matthew-1:

22. *Now all this was done, that it might be fulfilled which was spoken of the Lord by the prophet, saying, 23. Behold, a virgin shall be with child, and shall bring forth a son, and they shall call <u>His name</u> <u>Emmanuel,</u> which being interpreted is, God with us.*

Luke-2:

11. *For unto you is born this day in the city of David a Saviour, which is Christ the Lord.*

Matthew-1:

21. *"And she shall bring forth a son, and thou shalt <u>call His name JESUS: for He shall save His people from their sins.</u>"*

Luke-1:

35. And the angel answered and said unto her, The Holy Ghost shall come upon thee, and the power of the Highest shall overshadow thee: therefore also that holy thing which shall be born of thee shall be called the Son of God.

Isaiah-9:

6. For unto us a child is born, unto us a son is given: and the government shall be upon His shoulder: and His name shall be called Wonderful, Counsellor,The mighty God ,The everlasting Father, The Prince of Peace.

Zechariah-9:

9. "Rejoice greatly, O daughter of Zion; shout, O daughter of Jerusalem: behold, thy King cometh unto thee: He is just, and having salvation; lowly, and riding upon an ass, and upon a colt the foal of an ass.

Luke-2:

52. And Jesus increased in wisdom and stature, and in favour with God and man.

2) <u>HIS LIFE</u>

<u>Acts-10:</u>

38. How God anointed Jesus of Nazareth with the Holy Ghost and with power: who went about doing good, and healing all that were oppressed of the devil; for God was with Him.

<u>Isaiah-61:</u>

1. The Spirit of the Lord GOD is upon me; because the LORD hath anointed me to preach good tidings unto the meek; He hath sent me to bind up the broken hearted, to proclaim liberty to the captives, and the opening of the prison to them that are bound;

<u>Luke-4:</u>

18. "The Spirit of the Lord is upon me, because He hath anointed me to preach the gospel to the poor; He hath sent me to heal the brokenhearted, to preach deliverance to the captives, and recovering of sight to the blind, to set at liberty them that are bruised,"

Matthew-4:

17. *"From that time Jesus began to preach, and to say, <u>Repent:</u> for the kingdom of heaven is at hand."*

[<u>He will judge us</u> according to our works on this earth.]

Matthew-16:

27. **For the Son of man shall come in the glory of His Father with His angels; and then He shall reward every man according to his works.**

Isaiah-42:

1. *"Behold my servant, whom I uphold; mine elect, in whom my soul delighteth; I have put my spirit upon Him: He shall bring forth judgment to the Gentiles.*

Matthew-12:

18. *Behold my servant, whom I have chosen; my beloved, in whom my soul is well pleased: I will put my spirit upon Him, and He shall shew judgment to the Gentiles.*

<u>HE IS THE WORD OF GOD ALMIGHTY</u>

[JESUS-CHRIST-Who is the 'Word of GOD' sent to this Earth, to show us the way, this is needed to lead a perfect and a holy-life on this earth.]

John-1:

1. <u>In</u> the <u>beginning was</u> the <u>Word, and</u> the <u>Word was with God, and</u> the <u>Word was God.</u>
14. <u>And the Word was made flesh</u>, and dwelt among us, (and we beheld His glory, the glory as of the only begotten of the Father,) full of grace and truth.

Psalms-107:

20. "<u>He sent His word</u>, and healed them, and delivered them from their destructions."

Isaiah-55:

11. So shall my <u>word</u> be that goeth forth out of my mouth: it shall not return unto me void, but it shall accomplish that which I please, and it shall prosper in the thing whereto I sent it.

Jeremiah-22:

29. O earth, earth, earth, hear <u>the word of the LORD</u>

Matthew-4:

4. But He answered and said, It is written, Man shall not live by bread alone, but by _every word_ that proceedeth out of the mouth of God.

John-12:

47. And if any man hear my words, and believe not, I judge him not: _For I came not to judge the world, but to save the world._

49. "For I have not spoken of myself; but the Father which sent me, He gave me a commandment, what I should say, and what I should speak."

50. "_And I know that His commandment is life everlasting: whatsoever I speak therefore, even as the Father said unto me, so I speak._"

Luke-11:

28. But **He said,** yea rather, **Blessed are they that hear the _word of God_, and, and keep it.**

John-17:

8. For I have given unto them the words which thou gavest me; and they have received them, and have known surely that I

came out from thee, and they have believed that thou didst send me.
17. Sanctify them through thy truth: thy word is truth.

Proverbs-30:

5. Every word of God is pure: He is a shield unto them that put their trust in Him.
6. Add thou not unto His words, lest He reprove thee, and thou be found a liar.
[In order to straightened the false teaching]
Isaiah-40:

8. "The grass withereth, the flower fadeth: but the word of our God shall stand for ever.
Revelation-19:

13. "And He was clothed with a vesture dipped in blood: and His name is called The Word of God."

[JESUS CHRIST IS described in 'THE SCRIPTURE' as WORD of GOD-ALMIGHTY, SAVIOUR, Son of Man, THE BRANCH, 'THE SON OF THE LIVING-GOD, EMMANUEL-meaning-GOD with us, LAMB OF GOD, KING of KINGS, LORD of LORDS, SON Of MAN.He is the Light of the world, The Living water, Living Bread. Good-Shepherd. True Vine.]

LIGHT OF MEN

John-1:

4. *In him was life; and the life was the light of men.*
5. *And the light shineth in darkness; and the darkness comprehended it not.*
9. *That was the true Light, which lighteth every man that cometh into the world.*

John-8:

12. *Then spake Jesus again unto them, saying, I am the light of the world: he that followeth me shall not walk in darkness, but shall have the light of life.*

John-12:

46. *"I am come a light into the world, that whosoever believeth on me should not abide in darkness."*

Luke-2:

32. *"A light to lighten the Gentiles, and the glory of thy people Israel."*

John-9:

5. "As long as I am in the world, I am the light of the world."

Matthew-16:

15. He saith unto them, But whom say ye that I am?
16. And Simon Peter answered and said, Thou art the Christ, the Son of the living God.
17. And Jesus answered and said unto him, Blessed art thou, Simon Barjona: for flesh and blood hath not revealed it unto thee, but my Father which is in heaven.

John-1:

41. He first findeth his own brother Simon, and saith unto him, We have found the Messias, which is, being interpreted, the Christ.

John-4:

25. The woman saith unto Him, I know that Messias cometh, which is called Christ: when He is come, He will tell us all things.
26. Jesus saith unto her, I that speak unto thee am He.
29. Come, see a man, which told me all

things that ever I did: <u>is not this the Christ?</u>
42. And said unto the woman, Now we
believe, not because of thy saying: for we
have heard Him ourselves, <u>and know that this</u>
<u>is indeed the Christ, the Saviour of the world.</u>

John-11:

27. She saith unto him, Yea, Lord: <u>I believe</u>
<u>that thou art the Christ, the Son of God,</u>
<u>which should come into the world.</u>

Isaish-11:

1. And there shall come forth a rod out of the
stem of Jesse, and a <u>Branch</u> shall grow out
of his roots:
10. And in that day there shall be <u>a root of</u>
<u>Jesse,</u> which shall stand for an ensign of the
people; to it shall the Gentiles seek: and His
rest shall be glorious.

Zechariah-6:

12. And speak unto him, saying, Thus
speaketh the LORD of hosts, saying, Behold
the man whose name is <u>The BRANCH;</u> and he
shall grow up out of his place, <u>and he shall</u>
<u>build the temple of the LORD:</u>

<u>1 Corinthians-6:</u>

19. What? know ye not that <u>your body is the temple of the Holy Ghost</u> which is in you, which ye have of God, and ye are not your own?
<u>20. For ye are bought with a price: therefore glorify God in your body, and in your spirit, which are God's.</u>

<u>John-10:</u>

9. "<u>I am the door:</u> by me if any man enter in, he shall be saved, and shall go in and out, and find pasture."
11. "<u>I am the good shepherd: the good shepherd giveth his life</u> for the sheep.
15. As the Father knoweth me, even so know I the Father: and I lay down my life for the sheep.
27. My sheep hear my voice, and I know them, and they follow me:

<u>Ezekiel-34:</u>

11. For thus saith the Lord GOD; Behold, I, even I, will both search my sheep, and seek them out.

<u>Isaiah-53:</u>

6. *All we like sheep have gone astray; we have turned everyone to his own way; and the LORD hath laid on Him the iniquity of us all.*
<u>LAMB OF GOD, KING OF KINGS, AND LORD OF LORDS'</u>

<u>John-1:</u>

29. *The next day John seeth Jesus coming unto him, and saith, Behold the <u>Lamb of God,</u> which taketh away the sin of the world.*
34. *And I saw, and bare record that <u>this is the Son of God.</u>*

<u>Revelation-17:</u>

14. *These shall make war with the Lamb, and the Lamb shall overcome them: for <u>He is Lord of lords, and King of kings:</u> and they that are with Him are called, and chosen, and faithful.*

<u>Revelation-19</u>

16. *<u>And</u> He <u>hath</u> <u>on</u> His <u>vesture</u> <u>and</u> <u>on</u> <u>His</u> <u>thigh</u> a <u>name written,</u> <u>KING OF KINGS, AND LORD OF LORDS.</u>*

John-6:

33. "For <u>the bread of God is He</u> which cometh down from heaven, and giveth life unto the world."

35. "And Jesus said unto them<u>, I am the bread of life:</u> he that cometh to me shall never hunger; and <u>he that believeth on me shall never thirst."</u>

51. "<u>I am the living bread</u> which came down from heaven: if any man eat of this bread, he shall live for ever: and the bread that I will give is my flesh, which I will give for the life of the world."

Jeremiah-17:

13. "O LORD, the hope of Israel, all that forsake thee shall be ashamed, and they that depart from me shall be written in the earth, because they have forsaken the LORD, <u>the fountain of living waters."</u>

John-4:

14.But whosoever drinketh of the water that I shall give him shall never thirst; but the water that I shall give him shall be in him a well of water springing up into everlasting life.

<u>John-15:</u>

1. *"<u>I am the true vine</u>, and my Father is the husbandman.*

5. *"I am the vine, ye are the branches: He that abideth in me, and I in him, the same bringeth forth much fruit: <u>for without me ye can do nothing</u>."*

[JESUS CHRIST was sent to the earth not only to save us but also to end the ritualistic and pathetic animal sacrifice]

<u>Matthew-9:</u>

13. *But go ye and learn what that meaneth, I will have mercy, and not sacrifice: for I am not come to call the righteous, but sinners to repentance.*

<u>Proverbs-15:</u>

8. *The sacrifice of the wicked is an abomination to the LORD: but the prayer of the upright is His delight.*

<u>Hosea-6:</u>

6. *For I desired mercy, and not sacrifice; and the knowledge of God more than burnt offerings.*

Hebrews-7:

27. "Who needeth not daily, as those high priests, to offer up sacrifice, first for his own sins, and then for the people's: for this He did once, when He offered up Himself."

3) HIS DEATH

[Almighty-God gave His Son Jesus authority over the earth and death to save the Humanity as a whole, death is nothing but the separation of soul-from the body].

Hebrews-9:

22. "And almost all things are by the law purged with blood; and without shedding of blood is no remission."

26. For then must He often have suffered since the foundation of the world: but now once in the end of the world hath He appeared to put away sin by the sacrifice of himself.

Hebrews-10:

4. For it is not possible that the blood of bulls and of goats should take away sins.

18. Now where remission of these [is, there is] no more offering for sin.

<u>Matthew-26:</u>

28. *For this is my blood of the new testament, which is shed for many for the remission of sins.*

<u>John-8:</u>

28. *Then said Jesus unto them, When ye have lifted up the Son of man, then shall ye know that I am He, and that I do nothing of myself; but as my Father hath taught me, I speak these things.*

[We have to acknowledge that <u>JESUS CHRIST is sent</u> to this earth by His Father 'The Almighty-God' for the <u>remission of our sins</u>].

<u>saiah-53:</u>

5. *But He was wounded for our transgressions, He was bruised for our iniquities: the chastisement of our peace was upon Him; and with His stripes we are healed.*
6. *All we like sheep have gone astray; we have turned everyone to his own way; and the LORD hath laid on Him the iniquity of us all.*

7. He was oppressed, and He was afflicted, yet He opened not His mouth: He is brought as a lamb to the slaughter, and as a sheep before her shearers is dumb, so He openeth not His mouth.

John-15:

13. Greater love hath no man than this, that a man lay down his life for his friends.
14. Ye are my friends, if ye do whatsoever I command you.

John-17:

1. These words spake Jesus, and lifted up His eyes to heaven, and said, Father, the hour is come; glorify thy Son, that thy Son also may glorify thee:
2. As thou hast given Him power over all flesh, that He should give eternal life to as many as thou hast given Him.4. I have glorified thee on the earth: I have finished the work which thou gavest me to do.
5. And now, O Father, glorify thou me with thine own self with the glory which I had with thee before the world was.

<u>Luke-22:</u>

19. "And He took bread, and gave thanks, and brake it, and gave unto them, saying, This is my body which is given for you<u>: this do in remembrance of me.</u>"
20. "Likewise also the cup after supper, saying, This cup is the new testament in my blood, which is shed for you."

[Judas went to betray Jesus for mere thirty pieces of silver].

<u>John-13:</u>

2. "And supper being ended, the devil having now put into the heart of Judas Iscariot, Simon's son, to betray Him;"31. "Therefore, when he was gone out, Jesus said, Now is the Son of man glorified, and God is glorified in Him."

<u>Acts-26:</u>

23. That Christ should suffer, and that He should be the first that should rise from the dead, and should shew light unto the people, and to the Gentiles.

John-10:

17. Therefore doth my Father love me, because I lay down my life, that I might take it again.

18. No man taketh it from me, but I lay it down of myself. I have power to lay it down, and I have power to take it again. This commandment have I received of my Father.

Mark-14:

36. "And He said, Abba, Father, all things are possible unto thee; take away this cup from me: nevertheless not what I will, but what thou wilt."

Luke-24:

7. Saying, The Son of man must be delivered into the hands of sinful men, and be crucified, and the third day rise again.
[God was against the hypocrisy of the so-called religious leaders]

John-5:

16. And therefore did the Jews persecute Jesus, and sought to slay Him, because He had done these things on the sabbath day.

18. Therefore the Jews sought the more to

kill him, because He not only had broken the sabbath, but said also that God was His Father, making Himself equal with God

Matthew-12:

6. But I say unto you, That in this place is one greater than the temple.
7. But if ye had known what this meaneth, I will have mercy, and not sacrifice, ye would not have condemned the guiltless.
8. For the Son of man is Lord even of the sabbath day.

Matthew-26:

59. Now the chief priests, and elders, and all the council, sought false witness against Jesus, to put Him to death;

Matthew-27:

24. When Pilate saw that he could prevail nothing, but that rather a tumult was made, he took water, and washed his hands before the multitude, saying, I am innocent of the blood of this just person: see ye to it.
25. Then answered all the people, and said, His blood be on us, and on our children.

Luke-24:

20. And how the chief priests and our rulers delivered Him to be condemned to death, and have crucified Him.

Mark-15:

24. And when they had crucified Him, they parted His garments, casting lots upon them, what every man should take.

25. And it was the third hour, and they crucified Him.

Luke-23:

34.Then said Jesus, Father, forgive them; for they know not what they do. And they parted His raiment, and cast lots.

Matthew-27:

35. And they crucified him, and parted his garments, casting lots: that it might be fulfilled which was spoken by the prophet, They parted my garments among them, and upon my vesture did they cast lots.

1 Peter-2:

24. Who His own self bare our sins in His own body on the tree, that we, being dead to sins, should live unto righteousness: by whose stripes ye were healed.

25. For ye were as sheep going astray; but are now returned unto the Shepherd and Bishop of your souls.

4) <u>RESURRECTION</u>

[The significance of JESUS-CHRIST's resurrection is nothing but an assurance to man-kind by our CREATOR that <u>truth prevails</u> and <u>an eternal-life</u> to those who follow <u>HIS COMMANDMENTS</u>].

<u>John-11:</u>

25. Jesus said unto her, I am the resurrection, and the life: he that believeth in me, though he were dead, yet shall he live:

<u>Isaiah-25:</u>

8. <u>He will swallow up death in victory</u>; and the Lord GOD will wipe away tears from off all faces; and the rebuke of His people shall He take away from off all the earth: for the LORD hath spoken it.

9. And it shall be said in that day, Lo, this is our God; we have waited for Him, and He will save us: this is the LORD; we have waited for Him, we will be glad and rejoice in His salvation.

<u>Luke-3:</u>

6. And all flesh shall see the salvation of God.

<u>John-5:</u>

24. Verily, verily, I say unto you, He that heareth my word, and believeth on Him that sent me, hath everlasting life, and shall not come into condemnation; but is passed from death unto life.

<u>1 Peter-1:</u>

3. Blessed be the God and Father of our Lord Jesus Christ, which according to His abundant mercy hath begotten us again unto a lively hope by the resurrection of Jesus Christ from the dead.

<u>Luke-9:</u>

56. For the Son of man is not come to destroy men's lives, but to save them. And they went to another village.

[We have to crucify our flesh that is earthly desires and seek 'The CREATOR' of this Universe, who is willing to give the desires of our heart, when we give Him the first place in our life.]

Luke-12:

29. And seek not ye what ye shall eat, or what ye shall drink, neither be ye of doubtful mind.

30. For all these things do the nations of the world seek after: and your Father knoweth that ye have need of these things.

31. But rather seek ye the kingdom of God; and all these things shall be added unto you.

Romans-8:

13. For if ye live after the flesh, ye shall die: but if ye through the Spirit do mortify the deeds of the body, ye shall live.

John-6:

63. It is the spirit that quickeneth; the flesh profiteth nothing: _the words that I speak unto you, they are spirit, and they are life._

[So the celebration is a continuous one by examining ourselves and obeying His laws as He obeyed His father-The Creator of this Universe].

John-8:

31. Then said Jesus to those Jews which beli eved on him, _If ye continue in my word,_ then are _ye my disciples indeed;_

32. _And_ ye shall _know_ the _truth, and_ the _truth_ shall _make you free._

<u>John-12:</u>

44."Jesus cried and said, he that believeth on me, believeth not on me, but on Him that sent me."

45."And He that seeth me seeth Him that sent me."

48. He that rejecteth me, and receiveth not my words, hath one that judgeth him: the word that I have spoken, the same shall judge him in the last day.

<u>John-17:</u>

5. And now, O Father, glorify thou me with thine own self with the glory which I had with thee before the world was.

6. I have manifested thy name unto the men which thou gavest me out of the world: thine they were, and thou gavest them me; and they have kept thy word.

8. For I have given unto them the words which thou gavest me; and they have received them, and have known surely that I came out from thee, and they have believed that thou didst send me.

John-14:

28. Ye have heard how I said unto you, I go away, and come again unto you. If ye loved me, ye would rejoice, because I said, I go unto the Father: for my Father is greater than I.

Matthew-12:

50. For whosoever shall do the will of my Father which is in heaven,the same is my brother, and sister, and mother.

Matthew-24:

35. Heaven and earth shall pass away, but my words shall not pass away.

Matthew-22:

37. Jesus said unto him, Thou shalt love the Lord thy God with all thy heart, and with all thy soul, and with all thy mind.
38. This is the first and great commandment.

2 John-1:

6. And this is love, that we walk after His commandments. This is the commandment, That, as ye have heard from the beginning, ye should walk in it.
7. For many deceivers are entered into the

world, who confess not that Jesus Christ is come in the flesh. This is a deceiver and an antichrist.

9. Whosoever transgresseth, and abideth not in the doctrine of Christ, hath not God. He that abideth in the doctrine of Christ, he hath both the Father and the Son.

10. If there come any unto you, and bring not this doctrine, receive him not into your house , neither bid him God speed:

John-20:

28. And Thomas answered and said unto him, My Lord and my God.

29. Jesus saith unto him, Thomas, because thou hast seen me, thou hast believed: blessed are they that have not seen, and yet have believed.

30. And many other signs truly did Jesus in the presence of His disciples, which are not written in this book:

31. But these are written, that ye might believe that Jesus is the Christ, the Son of God; and that believing ye might have life through His name.

[Let's remember that Christianity is not a mere label, but a way of life. As we strive to do the will of our Father in heaven, may we become the genuine, passionate, and wholehearted followers that Jesus calls us to be].

1John-5:

10. "He that believeth on the Son of God hath the witness in himself: he that believeth not God hath made Him a liar; because he believeth not the record that God gave of His Son."
11.And this is the record, that God hath given to us eternal life, and this life is in His Son.
12. He that hath the Son hath life; and he that hath not the Son of God hath not life.

[JESUS CHRIST is the only way to Heaven whom we have to obey His Commandments and acknowledge Him always].

1 John-2:

3. And hereby we do know that we know Him, if we keep His commandments.
6. He that saith he abideth in Him ought himself also so to walk, even as He walked.

<u>Proverbs 3:</u>

6. "In all thy ways acknowledge Him, and He shall direct thy paths.

[No one on this earth should say 'He is a foreign God. **He is neither a foreign God or a local God.** He is 'the son of the LIVING GOD, THE CREATOR of this Universe. 'The Gospel'-meaning-Good News which was given to the people of this earth by 'The Creator' of this Universe through His only begotten son Jesus Christ. He is called God because He is 'THE WORD' of The Creator Almighty God. He has spoken those that God Almighty wanted to convey to us.]

<u>John 12:</u>

49. "For I have not spoken of myself; but the Father which sent me, He gave me a commandment, what I should say, and what I should speak.
50. And I know that His commandment is life everlasting: whatsoever I speak therefore, even as the Father said unto me, so I speak."

<u>John-10:</u>

30. "I and my Father are one."

1 John-5:

7. For there are three that bear record in heaven, the Father, the Word, and the Holy Ghost: and these three are one.

1 John-4:

2. Hereby know ye the Spirit of God: Every spirit that confesseth that Jesus Christ is come in the flesh is of God:

Mark-8:

38. Whosoever therefore shall be ashamed of me and of my words in this adulterous and sinful generation; of him also shall the Son of man be ashamed, when he cometh in the glory of His Father with the holy angels.

Matthew-28:

19. "Go ye therefore, and teach all nations, baptizing them in the name of the Father, and of the Son, and of the Holy Ghost:"
20. "Teaching them to observe all things whatsoever I have commanded you: and, lo, I am with you alway, even unto the end of the world. Amen."

John-15:

*12. This is my commandment, That
ye love one another, as I have loved you.*

Revelation-21:

*4. And God shall wipe away all tears from
their eyes; and there shall be no more death,
neither sorrow, nor crying, neither shall there
be any more pain: for the former things are
passed away.*

Romans-6:

*14. For sin shall not have dominion over you:
for ye are not under the law, but under grace.*

Luke-24:

*46. And said unto them, Thus it is written,
and thus it behoved Christ to suffer, and to
rise from the dead the third day:47. And that
repentance and remission of sins should be
preached in His name among all nations,
beginning at Jerusalem.*

48. And ye are witnesses of these things.

*49. And, behold, I send the promise of my
Father upon you: but tarry ye in the city of
Jerusalem, until ye be endued with power
from on high.*

John-14:

16. *And I will pray the Father, and He shall give you another Comforter, that he may abide with you for ever;*

26. *"But the Comforter, which is the Holy Ghost, whom the Father will send in my name, he shall teach you all things, and bring all things to your remembrance, whatsoever I have said unto you."*

John-15:

26. *But when the Comforter is come, whom I will send unto you from the Father, even the Spirit of truth, which proceedeth from the Father, He shall testify of me:*

John-14:

23. *Jesus answered and said unto him, If a man love me, he will keep my words: and my Father will love him, and we will come unto him, and make our abode with him.*

27. *Peace I leave with you, my peace I give unto you: not as the world giveth, give I unto you. Let not your heart be troubled, neither let it be afraid.*

<u>Acts-1:</u>

9. And when He had spoken these things, while they beheld, He was taken up; and a cloud received Him out of their sight.
10. And while they looked stedfastly toward heaven as He went up, behold, two men stood by them in white apparel;
11. Which also said, Ye men of Galilee, why stand ye gazing up into heaven? this same Jesus, which is taken up from you into heaven, shall so come in like manner as ye have seen Him go into heaven.

<u>Mark-16:</u>

19. So then after the Lord had spoken unto them, He was received up into heaven, and sat on the right hand of God.

<u>Hebrews-12:</u>

2. <u>Looking unto Jesus the author and finisher of our faith; who for the joy that was set before Him endured the cross, despising the shame, and is set down at the right hand of the throne of God.</u>

<u>JESUS CHRIST IS COMING AGAIN to JUDGE.</u>

Revelation-22:

12. "And, behold, I come quickly; and my reward is with me, to give every man according as his work shall be."

Mark-13:

26. And then shall they see the Son of man coming in the clouds with great power and glory.

Revelation-1:

3. Blessed is he that readeth, and they that hear the words of this prophecy, and keep those things which are written therein: for the time is at hand.

7. Behold, He cometh with clouds; and every eye shall see Him, and they also which pierced Him: and all kindreds of the earth shall wail because of Him. Even so, Amen.

Revelation-22:

21. "The grace of our Lord Jesus Christ be with you all. Amen."

BLESSED AND PEACE-FULL CHRISTMAS TO ONE AND ALL

END NOTE

We are living in an uncertain world. Nobody knows what tomorrow holds for us. Nobody can predict tomorrow. Tomorrow never comes, unless God allows us to see that.

Proverbs-27:

1."Boast not thyself of to morrow; for thou knowest not what a day may bring forth.

[Let us be thankful and grateful for all His mercies.]

Psalms-103:

17. "But the mercy of the LORD is from everlasting to everlasting upon them that fear Him, and His righteousness unto children's children;"

So my next compiled-book is, **"From UNCERTAINTY To ETERNITY'** **which will cover the Promises of Almighty-God-The Creator and His love for His creation** to lead a sinless life through **His Son JESUS CHRIST.**

*I thank **ALMIGHTY-GOD**, and all those who helped me in completing this book.*

www.ingramcontent.com/pod-product-compliance
Lightning Source LLC
Chambersburg PA
CBHW031515150726

47990CB00007B/3039